Native Plants & Animals (pg. 22)

Food, Cult...

Famous People (pg. 41)

Major Cities & Attractions (pg. 44)

INTRODUCTION: HELLO FRIENDS!

Hola! My name is Gabby which is short for Gabriella, and I am from Mexico! I am 12 years old. I live on Isla Mujeres, which is an island in the state of Quintana Roo in Mexico. I like growing up on my little island. We have lots of fun. There is so much to do, like fishing, swimming, and diving. A lot of tourists visit my island to sit on the beach or see the sea turtles. There is even an old Mayan Temple on the island, which is beautiful and gives me a strong sense of my family's cultural background.

My house is not large, but it is the right size for my family. We have some chickens that lay the eggs that we eat. We also have a small vegetable garden in our yard where we grow squash, tomatoes, and other delicious food. My house has walls that separate our bedrooms and bathroom, but other than that, our house is open to the sun and sky. My favorite pet is my cat Alom, named after the god of the sky because he has blue eyes. My dog is a chihuahua named Lindo, which is the Spanish word for cute. Alom always sleeps on my bed with me, and Lindo has his own little bed next to mine.

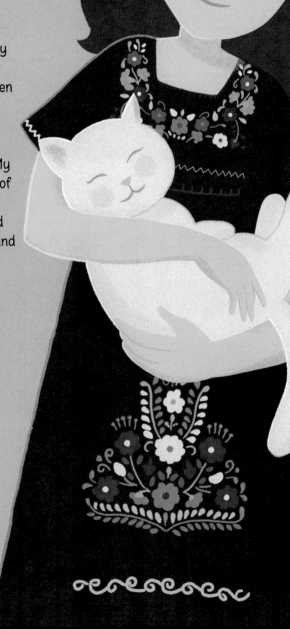

MEXICO
TRAVEL FOR KIDS

www.dinobibi.com

Author: Belinda Briggs
Editor: Kristy Elam
Illustrator: Teena Rahim

CONTENTS

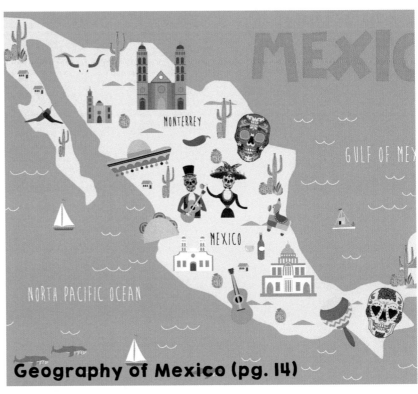

In Mexico, family is one of the most important things to us, if not the most important thing. My family is essential to me. I live with my mother, father, and my little brother. My grandparents also live with us. This might sound crowded to some folks, but we love it. My mother and grandmother cook most of our meals. I help them out a lot. I can help cook, and I can help mend clothing as well. As a family, we eat together at the same table. That means breakfast, lunch, and dinner, if we are in the house. Eating is not the only thing that we do together, though. We go on vacation together, we go to the beach together, and we spend holidays with our aunts, uncles, and cousins. My family is large, and we have deep roots in our community.

Isla Mujeres is the island that I live on with my family. The name means Women's Island, and I love that because my mother and my grandmother are my favorite people in the world. Both of my parents grew up on Isla Mujeres as did my grandparents. It is great living on an island. The weather is always warm here, and there is always something to do. I go to school here, too. Our school is small, but our teachers are very dedicated. Because of the warm weather, we often have our classes outside. My favorite subjects are art and science. I love art because so much of my cultural history has to do with art and because I enjoy painting and just being creative. I love science because I've grown up loving nature, and I want to be able to protect all animals that make my home so unique.

When I am not in school or at home with my family, I spend time with my friends from school. Sometimes we go hiking around our little island. If it's the right time of year, we can walk on the beaches and find sea turtle nests. We help protect those nests from poachers who sell the turtle eggs illegally and from birds and other animals that would eat them. The sea turtles are endangered, which is why we work hard to protect them.

Sometimes I volunteer at the Tortugranja (say tor-tu-gran-ya), the sea turtle farm on our island. At the turtle farm, we raise the little turtles until they big enough to take care of themselves, and then they will be released into the wild. The turtles are very important to my family and our culture because they have always been around, and we hope that they always will be. If people hunt them and eat their eggs, then that makes their chance of survival difficult. We believe all animals have just as much right to be on our planet as we do and not to be eaten!

I also enjoy swimming and snorkeling in the beautiful blue waters that surround my island. Isla Mujeres is on the Caribbean ocean, and I think that it is the bluest and most beautiful water in the world. In the water off the coast of my island live the most beautiful fish in the world, at least I think so! We also have sharks including, at certain times of the year, whale sharks, which are the largest fish in the world. Whale sharks are not dangerous; they eat the same things as blue whales and are no threat to us. I have even gone swimming with them. It is pretty amazing to be so close to such a giant creature!

My family and I observe our indigenous cultural traditions, and we also go to church on Sundays. My family and I dress up in our best clothes because the church is also a significant part of our culture and family life. My favorite dress is a traditional dress, which is a simple smock dress made of cotton and embroidered with flowers of every color. The flowers represent femininity and life. The colors reflect all the brightness around us. We also thank God when we are not in church, and we appreciate nature for all the beauty in our lives and all that we have.

Now that you know a little bit about me let me tell you about my country!

Before we continue our trip, I would like to know more about you.
Can you please complete this little questionnaire for me?

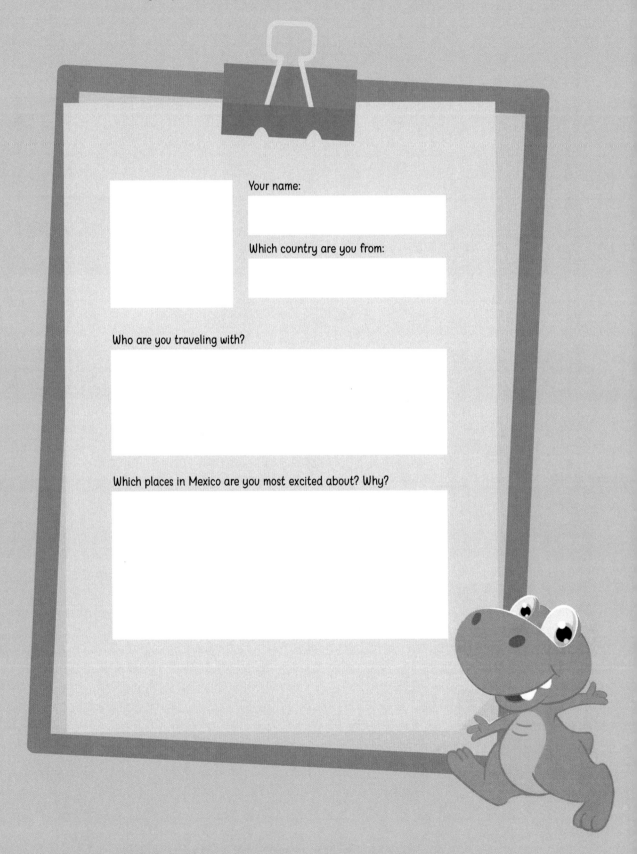

Your name:

Which country are you from:

Who are you traveling with?

Which places in Mexico are you most excited about? Why?

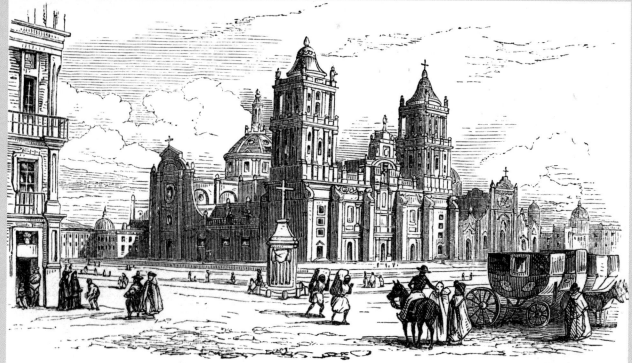

The Great Square and Cathedral, Mexico.

In Mexico, our history includes many different cultures. We didn't always speak Spanish. In fact, a long time ago, we spoke many different languages because our land had many different groups of people living on it, and each those groups had their own distinctive cultures.

Human culture in our area dates back 10,000 years, which is thousands of years before anyone arrived from Europe. Mexico is where we first domesticated and cultivated maize (corn), tomatoes, and beans. Those are still essential crops today, not just in Mexico but all over the world. Because of those crops, and the cultivation of them, different societies with their own cultures developed. Cities sprung up, and populations grew. With so many advances and social growth, early Mexico is one of the cradles of civilization, accompanying the Fertile Crescent in the Middle East, the Indo-Gangetic Plain in India, the North China Plain, and the Central Andes. At this time, most Mesoamericans are Nahua, which is the largest group of indigenous people in Mexico. Nahua is made up of many indigenous cultures who had their own customs and ways of life.

9

Our History Started a Long Time Ago!

The first known vast civilization in Mexico was a culture called the Olmec. The Olmec civilization developed and flourished in the fertile Gulf Coast at some point around 1500 BCE (BCE means Before Common Era). The Olmec people grew their civilization to become one of the first farming cultures. In that area, the rich volcanic soil was very fertile and combined with the regular rainfall and warm sun, this area was an excellent environment for growing crops. With crops growing abundantly, the society grew as well, so the Olmec people also developed large cities and social classes.

Olmec giant head sculpture carved from stone

Fun Fact

There are many different theories for why the Olmecs vanished. The most common is a combination of volcanic activity and the river basin becoming thick and dirty from farm runoff.

The Olmecs were probably the first culture in the Americas with a written language. The Olmecs are also credited with them as being the originators of the Mesoamerican calendar, sundials, and pyramids. And of course, it wasn't all work; the Olmecs were also the inventors of popcorn and the Mesoamerican ballgame which is one of the oldest sports in the world, and the oldest game using a rubber ball.

The Olmecs were also excellent sculptors, and their artwork is well known both for its style and size. They used tools made from stone and wood. Some of those tools can still be found in archaeological sites today! The giant Olmec heads are either sculptures of leaders of the society or possibly ballplayers. Unfortunately, the Olmec civilization eventually disappeared.

The Mayan Civilization

People believe the Mayan civilization developed from the Olmecs around 2000 BCE. While it is true that they have a lot in common, the Mayans were also very different. The Mayans continued the use of the calendar originated by the Olmec people. The Mayans were more expansive, and their territory expanded from Southeastern Mexico to include parts of Guatemala and Belize as well as parts of Honduras and El Salvador. The Mayans are best known for their writing system, which was the most developed in all the ancient Americas. The Mayans made many advances, including their cities which were actually more like the Roman City States, each having its own government and interests. The Mayans created their famous calendar, called the Mayan or Mesoamerican Calendar, one of the most complex, yet accurate, known. The Mayans also built pyramids and were great sculptors. Unfortunately, with so many city-states war often broke out, leading cities to be abandoned, which caused a decline in their civilization.

Maya glyphs, writing system, and languge

The Aztec Empire

Possibly the most well-known ancient Mexican Civilization was the Aztec Empire. People generally think of the Aztecs as one group of people. In actuality, the Aztec Empire is more appropriately called the Triple Alliance which was comprised of the three different Nahua city-states Mexico: Tenochtitlan (say Teh-Notch-tit-lan), Texcoco, and Tlacopan (say La-co-pan) who together conquered other lands and peoples. The Aztec Empire ruled from around 1428 CE to 1521. The Aztec ruled their conquered lands much the way ancient Rome did, allowing the rulers of the people that they defeated to stay in power as long as those people paid tribute yearly and contributed to the Aztec military in times of war. By ruling this way, the Aztecs grew in power and wealth. The Aztecs were not only wealthy and powerful, but they also grew in culture. In addition to art and architecture, the Aztec people had printed books. The last Mexican Emperor was Montezuma II. The Spanish led by Hernan Cortes and an army made up of both Spanish soldiers and soldiers from the other indigenous peoples conquered by the Triple Alliance finally conquered the Aztecs.

MUTECZUMA

Rex ullimus Mexicanorum

Moctezuma II (c.1465-1520), Aztec ruler

11

Spanish Rule and Influence

After the Spanish took control of Mexico, they renamed the land 'New Spain.' Under Spanish rule, Mexico grew to a booming area for trade, exporting many goods, including silver as the demand grew. Mexico City, which was the capital of New Spain, was the 'first world city' similar to today's New York or Hong Kong because materials were sold and traded there from all over the world. At this time, Mexican pesos became the first world currency, traded across the globe. Under Spanish rule, Mexico became cosmopolitan and was the home of the Americas' first print house, public library, public park, and the first university. At that time, Mexico was so rich that Spain used that wealth to trade and wage crusades all over the world.

Additionally, the US state of California was part of New Spain along with Texas and New Mexico. During the colonial period under Spanish rule, art, literature, and even food flourished as the European Spanish and indigenous cultures combined. Unfortunately, a lot of our indigenous culture was stifled under Spanish rule in favor of European culture and the dominant religion of Christianity.

Fun Fact

Over seventeen different indigenous groups lived in Mexico. Some still do.

Mexican Flag

Mexico's flag is very much a throwback to her indigenous people's religions. The green represents hope, white represents purity, and red is for the blood of those who sacrificed their lives for Mexico. The eagle eating the snake is from the ancient Aztec symbol for Tenochtitlan.

Independence

Colonized Mexico wanted independence to rule ourselves. In 1810, the Mexican people revolted against the occupying Spanish. Some of the Spanish living in Mexico joined the fight in support of the revolutionaries. Finally, Mexico declared its independence in 1821. That was just the beginning, though. As parts of the US states of Texas, California, Arizona, and New Mexico were part of our territory, at that time, Mexico was not only wealthy, but it was one of the largest countries in the world. Our nation was reborn the United States of Mexico, and after about twenty years, we developed into the constitutional republic.

Due to the disruptions in our political structures the northern territories at the time, Texas, Alta California (upper or north California) which is today's California, Arizona, Texas, and New Mexico were neglected when it came to governmental services and trade but were still expected to pay taxes, so they revolted. The Mexican-American War began in 1846, starting when the USA annexed Texas. After two years of war in 1848, the Treaty of Guadalupe Hildago was signed ending that war and giving the USA four new states. Additionally, in 1947, we had more political unrest leading to a new constitution and a secular federal government. We are still a secular government today.

There is a saying that tells us that democracy is a work in progress that is forever changing. I believe that this is true. My country has been around for many years. Some of those years have been good, some not so much. But we are still here today. Mexico is a beautiful and old country. We have had many changes over the years. I am proud of the history and growth of my country. We know how we came to where we are now, and I look forward to seeing where we will go.

Fun Fact
The poinsettia flower is named for Joel Roberts Poinsett who was the first US ambassador to Mexico.

El Angel - Mexican Independence Monument in Mexico City

GEOGRAPHY IN MEXICO

Mexico is the fifth largest country in the American continents! We have thirty-one states, including my home state of Quintana Roo! Mexico has many cities and towns; some are big, some are smaller. We also have a very diverse landscape that includes tall mountains, rainforests, fabulous beaches on both our Pacific and Caribbean coasts as well as the Gulf of Mexico. We even have some desert areas!

In Mexico, we hold a pretty important place in our part of the world. Up north, we border the USA. Just south of us are the countries of Guatemala and Belize. To our west is the Pacific Ocean, and our east coast touches the beautiful blue Caribbean Sea. We share a lot, like cultures and trade, with those three coastal countries.

Cancun beach during summer

31 States

Because we are such a big country, we have a lot of states (thirty-one to be exact) and each of those states contributes something essential to our country and to the world! Some of our states are well-known, including my state Quintana Roo (say kuin-tana - roo). Quintana Roo is best known for being the home of some of Mexico's most beautiful beaches, including Cancun. Cancun is not just a place for beautiful beaches, it is also a big city with lots of culture and a very popular spot for people all over the world to visit on vacation.

Chihuahua (say Chi-waa-waa) is our country's largest state, and we are proud it is the origin of the world's smallest dog also called a chihuahua! Baja California (say ba-ha) borders the state of California but is not a part of that US state. The word 'Baja' is Spanish for 'lower' so actually the name of that state means 'lower California' which is what this state was called all the way back in 1804 when it was still Spanish territory. Baja California is also an excellent place for surfing and some super rad beaches. Just south of Baja California is Baja California Sur. Sur means south so that name is sort of self-explanatory! We even have a state named Mexico, so if you are going to travel there you would be going to Mexico, Mexico!

Nevado de Toluca, Trans-Mexican Volcanic Belt, Mexico

Our Regions!

Our geographic regions are super diverse! Have you ever seen a desert? We have deserts with tons of sand and cactuses. Mexico's largest desert is in Chihuahua. Our other deserts include the Sonora Desert, which we actually share with the US states of California and Arizona, and both Baja California and Baja California Sur share the Baja California desert.

Chihuahua desert at the US border

Forests and Beaches!

Aerial of a Mexican forest with road, Mexico

Speaking about forests, we have an extraordinary place called the Monarch Butterfly Biosphere Reserve. That's right, there is a forest area devoted to the protection of butterflies, specifically the monarch which migrates from the northeastern side of the USA down to Mexico to spend the winter months. This place is dedicated not just to conserving the butterflies but also to protecting their habitat because we all need a place to live!

If you like hiking through a jungle, let us not forget our rainforests! Yes, we have rainforests which are home to all sorts of amazing and beautiful birds, reptiles, and furry mammals! Our most famous rainforest area is Lacandon Jungle, on the southern part of the Yucatán Peninsula. Like all rainforests, it requires protection because of human development and poaching. It is the largest rainforest in North America. If you are lucky, you might see a jaguar! In Lacandon, we also can find monkeys, parrots, and coatis, among other fun and unique animals.

If a damp rainforest is not for you, we have dry forests which are more on the Pacific side because nothing on the east coast is dry! Do you know what a cloud forest is? A cloud forest is a magical place high up in mountain areas where it is very humid, and the air temperature is cooler causing clouds that seem to be lower (even though the altitude is high). And we have enchanting cloud forests. In cloud forests, you can find all sorts of unusual plants, including orchids! Cloud forests are enchanting and mysterious. Even the air seems magical there.

Monarch Butterflies on tree branch at the Monarch Butterfly Biosphere Reserve

Lakes and Rivers

Early Morning Along the Rio Grande

In addition to our oceans, we have lots of fresh water bodies of water all over. We have large lakes and gallons of rivers that wind their way through our country, some of them even come south from the USA! Our two most famous rivers are the Rio Grande (Great River) and the Colorado River, or Rio Colorado. The Rio Grande actually starts in the Southern part of the US state of Colorado and works its way all the way to the border of the USA and Mexico. The Colorado River also begins in the state of Colorado in their Rocky Mountains and winds its way down to our states, Baja California and Sonora. If you enjoy riding rapids, these two rivers are for you! But those are only two rivers, and we have twenty-six of them!

Fun Facts About Mexico's Geography

The Chihuahua is the world's smallest dog. It's true, they are smaller than most people's house cats!

Mexico ranks first in the Americas and Seventh in the world for the amount of UNESCO World Heritage Sites.

Mexico is the thirteenth largest country in the world.

Chapala Lake

If you love calm and tranquil lakes, we are rich in those as well! Lake Xochimilco (say So-chi-milk-o) is an extraordinary place because it is the only remaining habitat for a severely endangered amphibian called an axolotl. Lake Xochimilco is an ancient lake that is between 6,000 and 12,000 years old! The axolotl is sort of like a salamander and can regenerate many of its body parts including arms, legs and even some parts of their brains! Since Lake Xochimilco is the only place where these animals live, it makes this lake very important indeed!

Axolotl

Our largest lake is Lake Chapala which is on the border of our states of Jalisco (say Ha-lees-kaw) and Michoacan (say Meech-wah-kahn). This lake is home to many endangered and threatened fish and birds. Lake Chapala is also a stopping place for birds that migrate south to escape the winters in the northern United States.

These are only a few interesting places in our geographically diverse country! There are so many fascinating and beautiful aspects in my Mexico that it would take me days to mention them all. I will leave that to young explorers to discover. I hope that you can come to visit and explore here. I know that you will think Mexico is as beautiful a land as I do!

I love living in Mexico. It is my favorite country in the world. Of course, since I am only twelve years old, and haven't been anywhere else, I don't have a lot to compare it to. I love living on my island, and I love visiting my family members who live in other parts of Mexico. I love the different climates in Mexico.I love living in Mexico. It is my favorite country in the world. Of course, since I am only twelve years old, and haven't been anywhere else, I don't have a lot to compare it to. I love living on my island, and I love visiting my family members who live in other parts of Mexico. I love the different climates in Mexico.

Cardon Cactus Desert in Baja California

It Can Get Hot and Cold!

While typically when people think of Mexico, they think of warm and even hot temperatures. For the most part, that is true, but we also have places where it can get pretty cold. And we even have mountains that are so high that snow falls there. Those are mostly up north (well north in Mexico). In the mountain ranges, while the air can still be warm, the altitudes are so high that even though it is mild throughout most of my country, it can be cold and snowy up there. So, if you are planning on mountain climbing in Mexico, I encourage you to pack some warm clothes!

While Mexico tends to be warm, there are different types of warm weather. In the desert areas, for example, we have a hot desert and cold desert. Those can be found in the states of Baja Mexico, Sonora, Chihuahua, and Coahuila and mostly close to the border we share with the United States. There it can be scalding hot (up to 52.5 C/126.5 F) during the daytime but can become quite chilly in the nighttime. Our desert is not made up of only sand though as is often thought of desert areas. While there is lots of sand and hard soil, there is plenty of scrub plant life and, of course, cactuses!

The Caribbean Coast

On the Caribbean side, we tend to get more rain, especially on our southernmost part of Mexico, where you will find our rainforest and its wealth of wildlife. More rain is no problem though because you cannot have a rainforest without rain! My island of Isla Mujeres, Quintana Roo gets a good amount of rain and a lot of sun, which means we have a decent climate for growing fruits and vegetables in our little garden. Our coast (and my island) tends to have more humidity, and we get warmer air thanks to the warm Caribbean waters.

The Pacific Coast

Our Pacific coast is also dry but is more like a savannah, not as dry as a desert but has more of a rainy season and a dry season. During the rainy season, we get a lot of rain, and during the dry season, we get almost no rain. The Pacific Ocean is colder, and as a result, they get cooler summer temperatures, well, relatively cooler, thanks to the fresh air blowing in from the ocean and hot, dry summers with more cooling breezes.

Rainy forest in Gulf of Mexico

Rain

Our rainfall varies throughout Mexico. In the northern regions, we get a little less, especially in the desert, but in some parts, we can get up to 26 inches or 666 millimeters. The center of Mexico receives less rain overall with rain only 110 days out of the year total in the case of Puebla, but in Veracruz, the average rainfall has been 67 inches or 1719 millimeters which can cause flooding. Naturally, on the coasts and near lakes it rains more. Our Pacific coast can receive up to 64 inches/1641 millimeters of rain in places like Puerto Vallarta during the rainy season. The Caribbean coast tends to receive more significant rainfall with 78 inches/1975 millimeters in places like Villahermosa.

All in all, my country is warmer than in most of North America. But just like everything else in Mexico, our weather is diverse!

Fun Facts About Mexico's Climate

Tabasco receives more rain on average than any other part of Mexico receiving about 94 inches/2406 millimeters.

Baja California Sur is the driest part of Mexico receiving only about 7 inches or 176.2 millimeters of rain per year.

Mexico's busiest tourist season is from December to April when we, on average, receive almost no rain in some parts.

NATIVE PLANTS & ANIMALS

Puma

I love animals and being in nature, so I am pleased to say that Mexico is particularly rich in flora and fauna! I am so proud because my Mexico is the number four country in biodiversity, which means many different species live here. In fact, Mexico is listed among the seventeen megadiverse countries. That means that we have a mega amount of biodiversity! Mexico has several national animals. The golden eagle is our national bird, the jaguar is our national mammal, the sea turtle is our national reptile.

Mexican iguana in Tulum in Riviera Maya

Coatis

Megadiversity

We are a megadiverse country because while Mexico is part of North America, it also borders Central American countries that are more tropical. The USA and Canada are to our north (far north in the case of Canada), and more tropical lands like Guatemala and Belize to our south. We kind of have the best of both worlds. We have animals and plants that are indigenous to North America like wolves and whitetail deer, and we also have animals that live in tropical environments such as coatis, iguanas, and parrots. Since a lot of birds and other animals migrate south from North America to spend the winter, Mexico is a stop on their paths down south. In other words, when it comes to wildlife, we have it all!

Land Diversity

Since Mexico is a large land mass with islands, we have a lot of different types of habitats for very diverse groups of animals to live. In the northern part of Mexico, we share a lot of animal species with the southern USA such as pumas, hares, coyotes, various reptiles, amphibians, and birds. The southern borders we share a lot of central American animals including quetzals, jaguars, and of course more reptiles and birds.

23

Monkeys!

Our best-known monkeys are howler monkeys, and they live up to their name. They howl first thing in the morning, they howl when it is time to go to bed, they howl to express territory, and they howl when it rains! The name is pretty self-explanatory.

The howler monkey is the loudest land mammal in the world, and their howl can be heard up to three miles away! While the howls are loud and to some can be scary, the howler monkey is a peaceful vegetarian. Our other monkey is the spider monkey. The spider monkey lives in the rainforest and more difficult to spot because they tend to be shier. Howlers are less secretive, and while they seldom interact with humans, they are easier to see (and hear).

The Jaguar

Of all the animals that can be found in Mexico, by far one of the most important to our historic culture and that of most of Latin America is the jaguar! The jaguar has played a role in the ancient religions of most of Central and South America, including the Olmec, Aztec, and Mayan cultures. The jaguar can live in desert areas but is also very at home in the jungle and near the beach. The jaguar is the third largest cat in the world. Because the jaguar is a cat, it is a carnivore meaning that they only eat meat, so this animal is a hunter! Before Europeans came to the Americas, this cat ranged all over Latin America and parts of the southern United States. Since the twentieth century, the jaguars' numbers have declined because of habitat loss, and they are pretty much only seen from Mexico on south. The name jaguar comes from the Tupi (say too-pee) word meaning 'beast of prey' or large hunter. The jaguar also has the most powerful bite of any cat regardless of size. Jaguars hunt a wide variety of prey ranging from rodents to caiman and crocodiles to sea turtles. If you see one of these fantastic cats, consider yourself lucky!

Animals Only in Mexico

We have a few creatures that are endemic (only lives in one area) to Mexico. One such animal is the volcano rabbit. This bunny is the second smallest rabbit in the world, weighing at only about one pound. The volcano rabbit only lives in areas of the Trans-Mexican Neovolcanic Belt in higher elevations with specific grasslands and forests. This tiny rabbit is endangered because of human development and habitat loss. Since the volcano rabbit only lives in a particular place, by changing the environment by building homes and farms, humans have caused the little volcano rabbit to lose much of their original home range. These bunnies need habitat help!

The vaquita is another endangered animal that can only be found in Mexico. The vaquita is both the smallest and most endangered cetacean (aquatic mammals like whales and dolphins) in the world. Vaquitas only grow to four and a half feet long (about the same size as I am). Vaquitas only can be found in the Gulf of California, which is the body of water between the Mexican states of Baja California and Sonora. These tiny dolphins are endangered due to human encroachment on their particular habitat area, including the vaquitas becoming trapped in illegal gill-nets used by fishermen who are fishing for totoaba a critically endangered fish and also illegal to hunt. When vaquita become caught in the nets, they are unable to surface for air, and they drown. The vaquita is one of my favorite animals in the world, and I hope that we all do our best to save them.

Another unique animal that can be found only in Mexico is the fascinating axolotl (say Ah-ho-lot-teh). The axolotl is a particular type of salamander, also called the Mexican walking fish, although it is not a fish; it is an amphibian. The axolotl is unique and can only be found in Lake Xochimilco near Mexico City. Due to habitat loss, this little amphibian is in dire need of help. The axolotl isn't just cute (at least I think they are), the axolotl is a miracle of evolution and science because of their regeneration abilities. Axolotls can regenerate their arms, legs, gills, and even parts of their brains. Efforts are being made to clean up their habitat because they are very endangered, and if they do not receive help, they will become extinct.

Birds

While we are a favorite vacation spot of many migratory birds to escape the cold winters in the United States and Canada, we have some other very unusual birds of our own! The Mexican Parrotlet is a beautiful and charming little parrot only about five inches long. The males are bright green with turquoise on their wings and tail feathers, while the females and young are all green. They live in groups as they are very social, like the majority of parrots. Not only are they adorable, but they are also brilliant like most parrots with skills like problem-solving and using tools. They are endangered due to both the exotic pet trade and habitat loss.

Mexican Parrotlet

Hummingbird

We also have a wealth of hummingbirds. Hummingbirds are only native to the American continents. Hummingbirds are tiny birds usually only a few inches long, colored like gemstones, and some even appear to change their colors depending on the angle the sunlight shines on them. Hummingbirds are the only bird that can hover like a bee. Theirs wings beat on an average of 80 wingbeats per second in some species, and they have the highest metabolism of any warm-blooded animal. You can tell when one is around by the humming noise that they make when their wings flap, which is how they get their name! While hummingbirds can be found all over the various American continents, we have a few that are all our own. The Mexican hermit is a tawny color with a long tail and lives in the Pacific side of our country. The Oaxaca hummingbird lives in the southernmost part of the Sierra Madre del Sur in the state of Oaxaca. The turquoise crowned hummingbird, also known as Doubleday's Hummingbird lives on the Pacific coast of southwest Mexico.

Fun Facts About Mexico's Wildlife

Monarch butterflies fly nearly 3000 miles to spend winter in Michoacan, Mexico.

Mexico is home to six wildcats including the jaguar and puma. The other cats are smaller but just as important; they are the ocelot, margay, jaguarundi, and the Mexican bobcat.

Mexico is home to 717 species of reptiles, and 574 can only be found in Mexico! That is the world's most diverse collection of reptiles!

Those are just a few of the animals that can be found in Mexico. Mexico is a mega diverse country, which means that we have a wealth of wildlife. Sometimes you have to go to a specific area to find individual animals or birds, but it is always worth the travel. Anyone who loves animals would discover that Mexico is the place for them!

Our Plant Life in Mexico

I love Mexico's plant life. As a megadiverse country, we are not only rich in wildlife, but also in our plant life, which includes flowers, trees, fruits, and even cactuses. With so much wildlife, they all need food and homes. That is where all the flora comes in!

Naturally, we have quite a few plants and trees that can be found up north and down south. Mexico has deserts, rainforests, temperate forests, mountains, and coastal zones. We have diverse climates for different plants to live.

Our National Plants

Dahlia

Our national flower is the dahlia, which is indigenous to Mexico. The dahlia tubers were eaten by indigenous people before the Spanish arrival. The Aztecs not only used them as a food source but also used them medicinally including for the treatment of epilepsy. While some species of dahlia can be found in Guatemala and other parts of Latin America, the majority of the dahlia flowers are located in the mountainous forests of Mexico. The dahlia was chosen as the Mexican national flower in 1963 for its long history with Mexican culture.

If you think there is nothing so beautiful as a tree, our national tree is truly amazing. The national tree of Mexico is the ahuehuete (say Ah-way-way-tee) more commonly called the Montezuma Cypress. The ahuehuete is a tall semi-evergreen tree that grows near water bodies. This tree became our national tree because of its sacredness to indigenous Mexican culture. It plays a vital role in both Zapotec and Aztec creation stories. This tree has the honor of being the stoutest tree in the world, meaning it has a chubby trunk.

The most famous Montezuma Cypress is a tree named the Arbol del Tule on the grounds of the church of Santa Maria del Tule in the state of Oaxaca.

Cactuses

Various cactuses are also essential to us. The prickly pear cactus has a long history in Mexico for its medicinal properties and delicious flavor. In indigenous cultures, the fruit was used for digestive issues and anti-inflammatory properties. They also would use the fruit to dress wounds. Additionally, we get a gorgeous red dye that comes from an insect that feeds on the cactus.

Agave was one of the most critical plants in indigenous culture. This nutritious plant was an everyday food staple in Aztec culture plant and served many purposes. The spines were often used as needles for clothing production and medicine. The agave sap is very sweet and is used as a sweetener like sugar. Agave is also an ingredient in tequila, the alcoholic beverage that is most famous from Mexico.

Agave tequila landscape to Guadalajara, Jalisco, Mexico

29

Orchids

In Mexico, we have lots of orchids. Orchids are my favorite flowers. They can grow in the most challenging climates and are always beautiful and interesting. One of our favorite orchids that grows in Mexico is the Oncidium orchid. The Oncidium orchid has long stems with many little flowers that grow on those stems. The Oncidium orchid flowers look like little dancing ladies in fancy dresses and sometimes smell like chocolate or tangerines. If you like vanilla, then you enjoy a product that comes from one of our orchids! Vanilla comes from the vanilla orchid and was prized by the Aztecs who enjoyed the flavor. Orchids played a role in some indigenous cultures because of their color and beauty. They were symbols of femininity, fertility, and life.

Another one of my favorite flowers is the plumeria or more commonly named Frangipani flower. The plumeria grows on a twisty boney looking tree. The flowers come in a variety of colors ranging from a creamy yellow to red to pink. In Aztec and other indigenous cultures, this flower was associated with femininity and fertility and was also a symbol of wealth and status because it looks like a star and of course, smells amazing. If you are in Mexico and you see this flower, take time to stop and smell it because you won't regret it. In fact, you might be tempted to hold on to it and sniff it all day long!

Flowers in Our Culture

Sunflowers were also crucial to indigenous Mexicans because of so much of the culture related to the sun. For indigenous cultures, the sun was the giver of life. Our crops depend on the sun and the sun gives us warmth, light, and life to everything we need to survive. The sunflower was and still is held in high regard as the floral representative of that life-giving entity.

The poinsettia is probably our most famous plant even if most people don't know it originated in Mexico. This plant is commonly known as the Christmas flower as it is used to celebrate the holiday in many Christian cultures. In Mexico, indigenous cultures used it for its medicinal properties. It has anti-inflammatory properties and could also be used to reduce fevers. The poinsettia was also used to produce red dye for clothing.

In Mexico, flowers, plants and trees played an important role in indigenous life. They gave us food, shelter, medicine, and even color our clothing. Part of why Mexico is associated with bright colors is thanks to the colors we were able to get from those flowers. Knowing where our roots come from is essential, and Mexican roots grow deep and entwine with our plant life!

Fun Facts About Mexican Flora

Sunflowers and dahlias are actually made up of many tiny flowers called florets.

Both vanilla and chocolate were introduced to Europe from Mexico by Hernan Cortes. The Spanish added sugar to sweeten the bitter chocolate flavor. And we all know the history after that!

While the poinsettia has medicinal properties, it can also be irritating causing a rash or nausea, so keep your pets away!

FOOD, CULTURE, AND TRADITIONS

It is impossible to talk about Mexican culture as one culture. In fact, Mexico has many different cultures. While all of those cultures have similarities, they also have a lot of differences! While we all are Mexicans, we each have our own individual cultural ways. Some of us come from a farming culture, some from an indigenous culture, and some of us are a little bit of everything.

Our Family

One thing we all have in common in Mexico is that family is the most important thing to us. Our family does a lot together. This concept is typical all over my country. Family culture is not just respecting our parents, which I do of course! We eat nearly all of our meals together, we spend holidays with our family, and we even have neighborhood parties with our family. My grandparents live with us because it is important to take care of those who took care of us when we were younger. We celebrate every element of our families, old and young. And our traditions are mixes of Spanish and indigenous cultures because that is what we are.

Posadas During Christmastime in San Gregorio Atlapulco

Our Religions

Our dominant religion is Roman Catholicism, so most people in Mexico identify as Catholic, including my family. While we observe common Catholic holidays and traditions, we also have a few different ones as well. For example, we celebrate Christmas from December 12 through January 6. Those days are filled with celebration and festivals. I perform the posada with my other friends on the island. Each night, we travel around the neighborhood singing songs until we are invited in at which point, we have a party with snacks, games, piñatas (say pin-ya-ta) and fireworks. A different home invites us in each night. The posada represents the story of Mary and Joseph looking for a place to stay and give birth to Jesus. We receive gifts on January 6 which Día de Los Reyes (Day of the Kings referring to the three wise men) though depending on the family and home, we might also exchange a few gifts on Christmas Eve or Christmas Day.

Decorated tomb in the cemetery of Xoxocoatlan, Mexico

Our Unique Traditions

We are not limited to only observing Catholic holidays and traditions. Due to the majority of Mexican people having some indigenous heritage, many of us also observe traditions related to those backgrounds. One such custom that we keep is 'Dia de Los Muertos' which translates to 'Day of the Dead.' No, it is not a zombie party! It is a celebration of our loved ones who have passed on. This exceptional and unique tradition is an ancient tradition that can be traced back to the Aztecs. On this particular day, we believe the souls of our departed loved ones return from the underworld for a visit. During this day, we pay tribute to Mictecacihuatl (say meek-teka-see-watl) the goddess of the underworld and celebrate those loved ones by placing gifts on their graves, singing songs and dancing for them. We also decorate our homes with flowers and other bright and colorful items. It is our way of telling those souls that we still remember and celebrate them.

A related tradition that often accompanies Dia de Los Muertos is when we celebrate La Catrina, the lady of the dead. According to legend, La Catrina was a greedy, rich woman who refused to help those less fortunate than she was instead dressing in beautiful clothes and wearing fancy hats. The tradition of this celebration is to mock La Catrina by dressing in our finest dresses or other clothing, a large hat, and painting our faces to resemble a silly skull.

Guelaguetza celebration at Ocotlan Town Square

Another traditional indigenous celebration is Guelaguetza (say guay-la-guet-sa), which is my favorite tradition! This tradition is an old Zapotec one where we dress up in our most beautiful and most colorful clothing and dance. Guelaguetza translates to 'great courtesy,' and our dances are re-enactments of legends of villagers helping each other in times of need. It also to celebrate our hopes for good crops, especially corn. This tradition celebrates the idea of caring for the earth and each other. It also marks our enduring beliefs of kindness and respect for all life on our planet. I think that is why it is my favorite because it celebrates those two principles, which I believe are so important!

Fun Facts About Our Culture in Mexico

Modern day people of Mexico are actually a mix of Spanish, French, Zapotec, Olmec, Aztec, Maya, and Inca among other ancient civilizations.

Even though Spanish is the language associated with Mexico, in the more rural areas over fifty indigenous languages are still spoken.

During Mexican festivals our folk dances are celebrations of our European, African, and Indigenous heritage.

Our Cuisine

We cannot talk about Mexican culture without talking about food! When people who are not from Mexico think of Mexican cuisine, they usually think of tacos, burritos, and quesadillas. While I love all of those food items, I can honestly say that our food goes far beyond those staples! Mexico is diverse in our land and people. We have a very long history, and our menu reflects that!

How It All Began

Mexican cuisine goes far back to long before the Spanish colonized Mexico. It goes far before the Mayan and Aztec civilizations when indigenous people began to cultivate corn, about 9,000 years ago! Once they began to domesticate fruits and vegetables, the cuisine began to evolve. Remember, before any culture farmed food, they were hunters and gatherers. So, in fact, most civilizations started with the cultivation of food. In that respect, Mexico is no different. Mexico began with food!

Spicy Shrimp Tacos with Coleslaw and Salsa

Once different city states developed and began interacting and trading with one another, they were exposed to fruits and vegetables as well as herbs, spices, and even meats in addition to cooking methods that were not in their respective territories. Some foods that spread from one part of the region to another were turkey, beans, squashes, chocolate, avocados, tomatoes, and vanilla. As these foods spread from place to place as a result of trade. Folks used them in their own cooking, and as a result, people were exposed to new and delicious dishes.

Avocado dip guacamole with tortilla chips

Culinary Influences From Other Lands

When the Spanish conquered the Aztec Empire, they brought with them European food staples including domestic animals raised for meat including goats, pork, beef, and chickens. These meats provided the indigenous Mexican people with new food options to add to their own cuisines. In turn, the indigenous folk were able to share their staples such as corn, tomatoes, chocolate, and vanilla with the European settlers. With the Europeans also came slaves from Africa and Asia, which even further evolved the cuisine of Mexico to what it is today.

Beef burritos with rice, black beans, and salsa

Food In Our Culture

Our culture is not limited to religion. Our culture is also in our foods. Many of the foods we eat were eaten by our ancient relatives before the Spanish even thought of visiting our continent. Most of our food involves tomatoes, beans, corn, and vegetables. These foods are not just cuisine, they are important in ancient religions. Corn was considered sacred as were tomatoes. Our relatives would pray for good harvests and celebrate with gratitude when the crops were bountiful. We even grow tomatoes in our back yard!

I love being a mix of cultures. As a girl from Mexico, I can celebrate both modern traditions and our ancient traditions as well. I think that they are both extraordinary, and it is important to acknowledge both. I learn about our Mayan and Zapotec histories from my grandparents and even my Mom. Like most children in Mexico, I am proud of all my heritage.

All About Corn

Corn is one of the most essential foods on our menu. Since domesticating corn 9000 years ago, we have used it in many different forms. Corn can be eaten right on the cob, which is my favorite way, with a little butter and maybe a bit of salt. It can also be removed from the cob and added to salads, rice and beans, or just on its own. Another way of preparing corn is by drying and then grounding it into a flour, then using that flower to make breads, cakes, and tortillas, all of which play a significant role in our dining lives. Corn was so important to our ancient cultures that they even had gods, like Centeotl, devoted explicitly to it.

Beans, Beans, Beans

We do have certain food staples of our own today. In most meals, we will have beans and rice, which is a combination loved and eaten all over Latin America. Different regions prepare beans and rice in different ways. Sometimes it is simple, black beans and white rice, that's it. Other times, we add seasonings such as pepper or a delicate sauce made from tomatoes to it. And of course, we often add other things to it, such as corn, vegetables or a meat to as chicken. However you like it, rice and beans is filling, has a lot of protein and gives us the energy to face the day.

In Mexican culture, food is critical because it is a way of bonding with our family. Most of our meals are eaten together, and important holidays and festivals or celebrations often have specific foods associated with them. In Mexico, food brings people together. And we love to eat!

Fun Facts About Mexican Cuisine

The Spanish first added sugar to chocolate making it the confection that we know and love today!

Vanilla was spread all over Europe from Mexico!

Tomatoes originated in Mexico.

FAMOUS PEOPLE IN MEXICO

My country is the birthplace of many notable people, from artists and actors to musicians and rock stars to revolutionaries and activists. Regardless of if you love the arts and entertainment, or if you are interested in literature and music, or if your interests are in social and political issues, Mexico has it all!

Perhaps the most famous artist from Mexico is the amazing Frida Kahlo. She is often associated with the artist movement Surrealism, though she did not consider herself as a surrealist. Frida's art was very personal to her, exploring such themes of identity, ethnicity, and history. These topics were always on her mind because she had an ethnically diverse family background. Her father was German while her mother was of indigenous descent. She is most famous for her self- portraits depicting her in indigenous settings, traditional indigenous clothing, and wildlife that had indigenous symbolism. To this day Frida Kahlo is associated with the Raza (the folks of Mexico), the feminist movement, and diversity in all its forms.

Writers

If you are a fan of literature, we have contributed many notable authors to the world over the years. One of our most recent contributions to the literary world is the author Valeria Luiselli, whose works frequently raise awareness of the issues and feelings of immigrants to the United States in this modern time. As a court translator for immigrant children seeking asylum in the US, she heard many painful stories. Valeria also had some of those experiences herself as an immigrant, and those experiences combined with those of the children she worked with serve as material for her two most recent books in which she addresses the challenges and crises that cause people to leave their home countries in search of a safer life. Her works also discuss the challenging journeys immigrants make and the reception they receive at the border of the US and Mexico. Thanks to Valeria Luiselli, many people gain a more empathetic view for people who are seeking asylum in the US.

Actors

Mexico has contributed some wonderful actors to the global celebrity firmament! Salma Hayek is possibly the best-known actress from Mexico. She has been steadily acting since the 1990s. Salma Hayek has been nominated for multiple awards including Academy Award, Emmy Award, Screen Actors Guild award, and BAFTA award among others. Her acting roles have included comedies, dramas, and historical biographies. Salma Hayek is not only a talented actor, singer, and director, but she is also an activist for various causes including human rights, women's rights, and environmental conservation.

Our Musicians

We have a long and glorious musical history. We also have some very famous rock stars, hip hop artists, and even classical composers. Currently, our most renowned musician most likely would be Carlos Santana. Carlos and his band, Santana, rose to prominence in the 1970s, and Carlos still plays to sold out crowds today. As a musician, while he is a rock musician, he draws from a diverse range of Mexican influences including Latin jazz, indigenous music, and Mexican folk music as well as blues, reggae, and R&B. Santana is the recipient of 10 Grammy awards and more nominations. Carlos Santana is listed as one of the twenty greatest guitarists of all time and continues to play his music and collaborate with current artists to this day and hopefully will continue to for many years to come.

Fun Facts About our Famous Mexican people

Salma Hayek was nominated for an Academy Award for her portrayal of the Mexican artist Frida Kahlo.

Carlos Santana played at the famous 1969 Woodstock music and art festival even before his first album debuted.

The famous Mexican revolutionary Francisco 'Poncho' Villa was a bandit before he used his notable skills to fight for Mexico in the Mexican Revolution.

Those are some of our most famous people from beautiful Mexico. We have many more; with a country as big and diverse as Mexico it can't be avoided. Our country is filled with talent, passion, and ideas, and with some luck, some of those people with their ability, love, and thoughts become world famous!

MAJOR CITIES &ATTRACTIONS

CASAS DE Guanajuato

If you are visiting my country, you might wonder what to do. There a great many things to do and see here. We have entertainment for everyone, we have so much to do and see! If you love nature, we have a whole country full of wildlife of every sort. If you love history, we are an old country with a great deal of history and from different cultures! In Mexico, there is something for everybody!

In our big cities, including our capital of Mexico City, we have museums devoted to science, art, and history. You can see beautiful architecture to see and much history to experience. But, if you want to really experience Mexico, you have to leave the cities and get out into our country!

For Nature Lovers

For nature lovers, we have deserts, rainforests, temperate forests, grasslands, and even mountains. My two favorite places for wildlife are the Monarch Butterfly Biosphere Reserve and the Lacandon Jungle.

Butterflies

The Monarch Butterfly Biosphere Reserve is in the forested mountainous area about 100 km/63 miles Northwest of Mexico City. In this protected area of 56,259 ha/217 square miles, monarch butterflies arrive from the United States and Canada to spend the winter. They live on the trees, and people travel to this area to see how they literally turn the trees orange due to the amount of the insects covering the branches and foliage. I have never seen so many butterflies in one place. What makes this place even more special is that these butterflies are becoming endangered due to habitat loss from the destruction of their host plants for gardens and agriculture and other human development. This place is safe so they can continue to repopulate for future generations. If you live in an area where these butterflies are indigenous, a way that you can help them is by planting milkweed plants which they depend upon as both food and a place to lay their eggs. Not only will you see beautiful butterflies, but you will also see the most beautiful cocoons you can imagine; they look like beautiful blue and gold tiny pieces of pottery.

Rainforests

The Lacandon Jungle, or La Selva Lacandona, is our best-known rainforest. The Lacandon Jungle is the largest rainforest in North America (remember Mexico is considered North America) at about 1.9 million hectares (7336 square miles) total. This jungle is in the southwestern part of Chiapas and stretches into Guatemala. While much of the rainforest has been destroyed or damaged due to deforestation and human development, the protected area is still a sight to see. If you visit this fantastic rainforest, you will catch a glimpse of some of the animals that reside there including monkeys, agoutis, coatis, butterflies, parrots, hummingbirds and even, if you are fortunate, perhaps even a jaguar.

Small mayan ruins in the lacandon jungle of Chiapas Mexico

And of course, I must boast about my island! Isla Mujeres is a perfect spot to see sea turtles nesting. If you come at the right time, you might even be able to protect an erupting nest from predatory birds and crabs, helping the little turtles make their way to the sea! If you love snorkeling or scuba diving and are here at the right time, you can swim with whale sharks. Whale sharks are the largest fish in the world (their mouths alone can be over five feet wide) but don't worry, they are gentle giants, more like whales than sharks! If you visit my little island, please be mindful of our conservation policies, because those keep our island perfect, clean, and beautiful!

Famous historical ruins of Tulum in Mexico

Historic Places

If you are passionate about relics and history, we have plenty of museums, or you might visit one of our amazing archaeological sites! When attending an ancient place, I can't help but feel a powerful sense of history. I imagine how those people lived and what my country was like then.

Tulum is in the state of Quintana Roo (my state) and is the site of many excellent examples of ancient architecture. Tulum is the site of an ancient Mayan Wall that stretches 3–5 meters (9.8–16.4 ft) high. Here you can see examples of how skilled the Mayan stonemasons were. In Tulum, you can visit the Pyramid El Castillo (the castle) and other ruins as well as examples of Mayan artwork. By exploring this place, you can get a good idea of how this ancient civilization lived.

If you like more urban experiences, you should undoubtedly visit San Miguel de Allende. This municipality is located in the state Guanajuato and is situated about 274 km or 170 miles from Mexico City. This town has a great deal of history that ranges from before the Spanish rule and beyond. The city and Sanctuary are a UNESCO world heritage site.

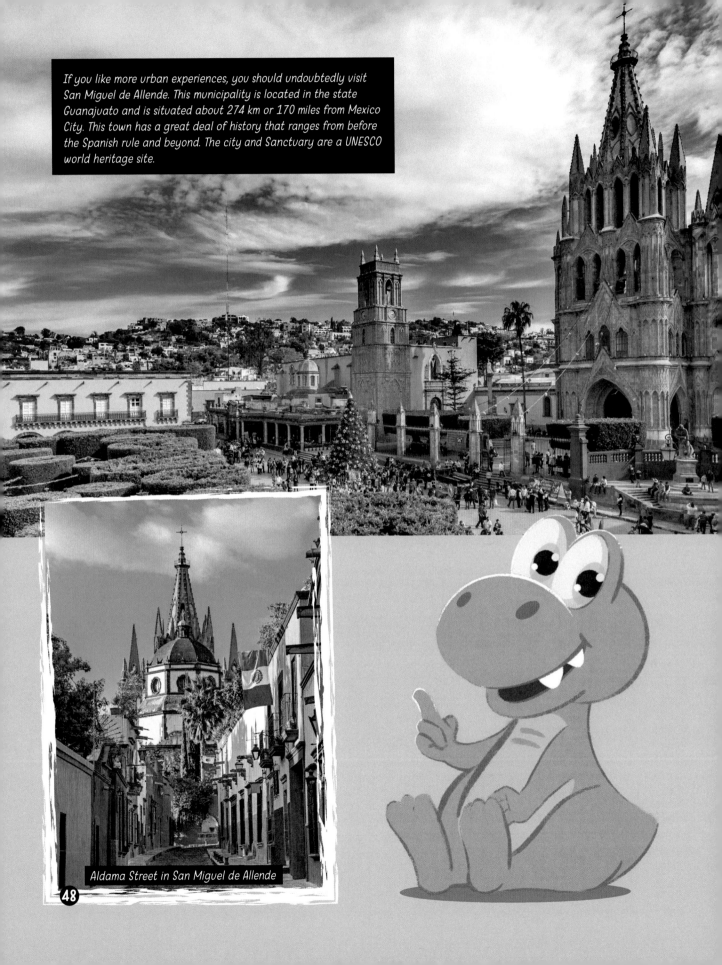

Aldama Street in San Miguel de Allende

My own island also boasts its own ancient history. The spot is sacred to the Mayan goddess Ixchel (say Ish-all) who was the Mayan goddess of childbirth and medicine, which is also why the Spanish named my island Isla Mujeres, or Island of Women. The temple is small and Hurricane Gilbert damaged it 1988, but it still is a great site to visit for a sense of ancient history.

Those are just a few examples of things that you can see in my country. Don't forget that Mexico is also home to spectacular beaches and beautiful waters. Of course, my favorite beaches are on the super blue Caribbean, but my country is vast, beautiful, and historic. You might want to stay for a while to see all that my country has to offer!

Fun Facts About Some Of Our Special Places

Mexico is home of over 30 UNESCO World Heritage Sites.

Mexico is home to the world's smallest volcano called the Cuexcomate volcano which is only 13 meters, or 43 feet tall, and 23 meters, or 75 feet in diameter.

Mexico City is sinking at about 10" per year because it was built on the remains of a lake.

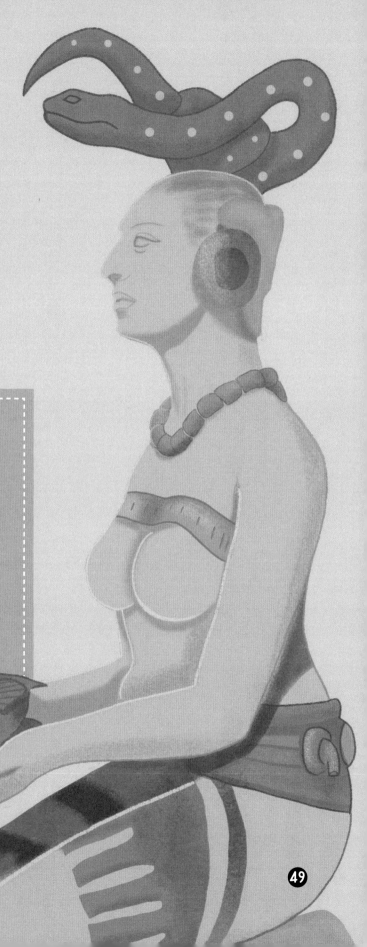

CONCLUSION

Mexico, is a big and beautiful country. I love growing up here and being Mexican. I love my country's history, culture, and life. There is so much to love about Mexico, from the exquisitely turquoise waters of the Caribbean, to our majestic rainforest which is home to some of the most magnificent animals in the world, to our mountains and lakes which nurture some of the rarest and unusual creatures. We have fantastic art and culture that draws influence from our history and the history of the world. Mexico is glorious, and I love it all. I know you will too, and I hope to see you in my country someday. Welcome to Mexico!

Which parts of Mexico did you like the most and why?

What activities did you enjoy most and why?

Now, to our pop quiz! Good luck!

The most famous ancient Mexican civilization is...?
a. The Aztec Empire or Triple Alliance.
b. The Apache civilization.
c. The Hun Civilization.

(answer (a) —The Aztec Empire or Triple Alliance)

Mexico is a part of _____.
a. North America.
b. South America.
c. China.

(answer (a) — North America.)

Mexico's deserts are in the states of _____.
a. Baja California, Sonora, Chihuahua, and Coahuila.
b. Quintana Roo, Baja Mexico Sur, and Tabasco.
c. Durango, Pennsylvania and Quintana Roo.

(answer (a) — Baja California, Sonora, Chihuahua, and Coahuila.)

Mexico is considered a _____country.
a. diverse
b. megadiverse
c. inverse

(answer (b) — megadiverse)

Mexico's National flower is the _____.
a. dahlia.
b. daisy.
c. Dendrobium orchid.

(answer (a) — dahlia)

In indigenous Mexican medicine, the prickly pear cactus was used for _____.
a. curing headaches.
b. fixing sunburn.
c. soothing digestive problems.

(answer (c) — soothing digestive problems.)

The cultures that make up Mexico are _____.
a. Shinto and Buddhism.
b. French and German indigenous cultures.
c. modern day Catholicism and traditional indigenous cultures.

(answer (c) — Catholicism and traditional indigenous cultures.)

Staples of traditional Mexican cuisine include_____.
a. corn, squash, and avocado.
b. cherries, apples, and bananas.
c. beef, chicken, and goats.

(answer (a) corn, squash, and avocado.)

The _____ is the largest rainforest in North America.
a. The Lacandon Jungle
b. The Amazon Rainforest
c. The Cardamom Mountains

(answer (a) — The Lacandon Jungle)

. _____ was the Mayan goddess of childbirth and medicine.
a. Ixchel
b. Alom
c Carruchan

(answer (a) — Ixchel)

I have thoroughly enjoyed this journey through Mexico with you.
Feel free to visit us at www.dinobibi.com and check out our other titles!

Dinobibi Travel for Kids

Dinobibi History for Kids

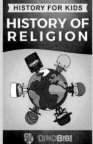

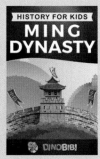

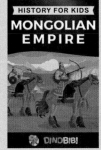

Made in the USA
Middletown, DE
20 August 2022

71846956R00031